This f*n Ph*nics reader

Ladybird Reading
Phonics
BOOK 8

Contents

A catalogue record for this book is available from the British Library

Published by Ladybird Books Ltd
80 Strand London WC2R 0RL
A Penguin Company

2 4 6 8 10 9 7 5 3 1
© LADYBIRD BOOKS LTD MMVI
LADYBIRD and the device of a Ladybird are trademarks of Ladybird Books Ltd

ISBN-13: 978-1-84646-318-1
ISBN-10: 1-84646-318-1

Printed in Italy

Joe's Showboat

by Irene Yates
illustrated by Eric Smith

introducing the common spellings of the
long **o** sound, as in coat, show and toe

Wherever Joe and his
steamboat go, the goats on
board put on a show.

Today, Joe's showboat
is a stuck-in-the-snow boat.

"Let's all row," says Joe.
But can they row the showboat?
No!

"Let's all tow," says Joe.
But can they tow the showboat?
No!

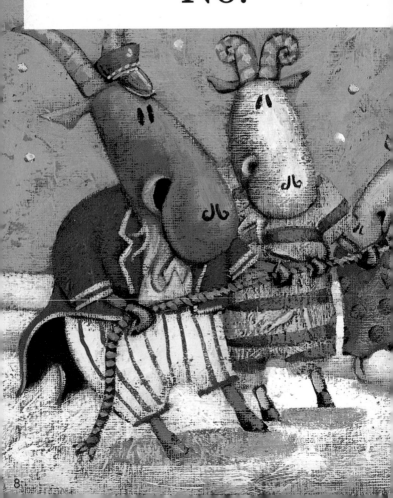

"I know!" says Joe. "We'll put on a show in the snow!"

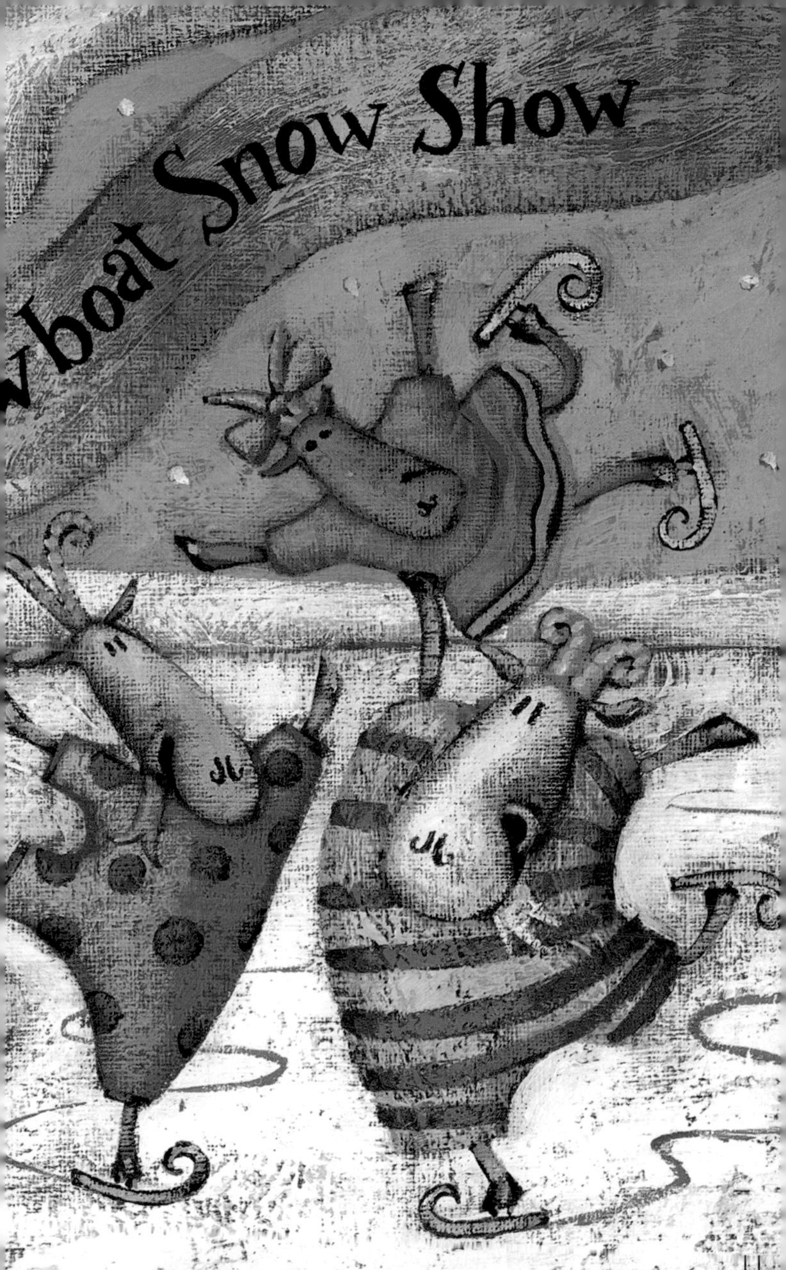
wboat Snow Show

tonight and
tomorrow only

Joe

~ and his ~

Showgoats

◆ present ◆

The Showboat
Snow Show

The Queen's Cream Tea

by Irene Yates
illustrated by Rosalind Beardshaw

introducing the common spellings of the
long **e** sound, as in sweet and dream

This is Queen Jean.

She is in a deep sleep.

Here is Queen Jean, in a
deep sleep, beneath a tree.

Here is Queen Jean, in a deep sleep, beneath a tree, by a peaceful stream,

dreaming a sweet dream.
Here is Doreen.

Here is Doreen with the Queen's cream tea.

Cream tea, your Majesty?

18

Here is a leaf in the breeze...

SN

EEZE!

Here are three
sheep in a heap.

Bless you,
your Majesty!

The Runaway Train

by Irene Yates
illustrated by Katy Taggart

introducing the common spellings of the
long **a** sound, as in train and play

Every day the midday train goes straight along the track.

It goes along the rails in wind or rain, then trails the same way back.

But on Monday, at the station,
the passengers all wait.

Today the daily midday train
is very, very late.

It's gone off the rails! It's puffing away! It's fed up of coming and going all day!

It's gone off the rails! It's sick of the strain of trailing along again and again.

So the runaway train is running away. It's running away for a holiday!

HURRAY!

HOW TO USE
Phonics
BOOK 8

This book introduces your child to the common spellings of the long a, e and o vowel sounds. The fun stories will help your child to begin reading words including any of the common spelling patterns that represent each of these sounds.

• Read each story through to your child first. Familiarity helps children to identify some of the words and phrases.

• Have fun talking about the sounds and pictures together – what repeated sound can your child hear in each story?

• Break new words into separate sounds (eg. h-ea-p) and blend their sounds together to say the word.

- Some common words, such as 'come', 'gone' and even 'the', can't be read by sounding them out. Help your child to practise recognising words like these.

- Talk about the letter groups as outlined on the title page of each story.

Phonic fun

Playing word games is a fun way to build phonic skills. Write down a list of three-letter words with vowels in the middle, like 'can', 'mad' or 'big'. Help your child to pick out the ones that can be made into new words by adding a final 'e'.

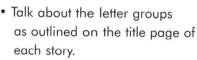

Help your child read the new words.

Ladybird Reading

Phonics

Phonics is part of the Ladybird Reading range. It can be used alongside any other reading programme, and is an ideal way to practise the reading work that your child is doing, or about to do in school.

Ladybird has been a leading publisher of reading programmes for the last fifty years. **Phonics** combines this experience with the latest research to provide a rapid route to reading success.

The fresh quirky stories in Ladybird's twelve **Phonics** storybooks are designed to help your child have fun learning the relationship between letters, or groups of letters, and the sounds they represent.

This is an important step towards independent reading – it will enable your child to tackle new words by sounding out and blending their separate parts.

How Phonics works

- The stories and rhymes introduce the most common spellings of over 40 key sounds, known as phonemes, in a step-by-step way.

- Rhyme and alliteration (the repetition of an initial sound) help to emphasise new sounds.

- Bright amusing illustrations provide helpful picture clues and extra appeal.